A Short-Te

INVITATION
TO
ROMANS

LEADER GUIDE

Abingdon Press

Nashville

A Short-Term DISCIPLE Bible Study

INVITATION TO ROMANS
LEADER GUIDE

Copyright © 2006 by Abingdon Press

Harriett Jane Olson, Senior Vice President of Publishing and Editor of Church School Publications; Mark Price, Senior Editor; Mickey Frith, Associate Editor; Kent Sneed, Design Manager; Leonardo M. Ferguson, Designer

Contents

Introducing
This Study Series

INVITATION TO ROMANS is one of a series of studies developed on the model of DISCIPLE Bible study. DISCIPLE is a family of Bible study resources based on the general assumption that people are hungry for God's Word, for fellowship in prayer and study, and for biblically informed guidance in ministry. Like all long-term DISCIPLE resources, this series of short-term DISCIPLE Bible studies: (1) presents the Bible as the primary text; (2) calls for daily preparation on the part of students; (3) features a weekly meeting based on small-group discussion; (4) includes a video component for making available the insights of biblical scholars to set the Scriptures in context; and (5) has as one of its goals the enhancement of Christian discipleship.

INVITATION TO ROMANS is designed to provide congregations with an in-depth, high-commitment Bible study resource able to be completed in a shorter time frame than the foundational DISCIPLE studies. However, the shorter time frame does not mean this study has expectations different from those associated with the thirty-four week DISCIPLE: BECOMING DISCIPLES THROUGH BIBLE STUDY. In fact, the term *invitation* rather than *introduction* has been used for this series to signal that these studies are not basic introductions but rather invitations to in-depth study. The expectation remains that participants will prepare for the weekly meeting by reading substantial portions of Scripture and taking notes. The expectation remains that group discussion, rather than lecture, will be the preferred learning approach. The expectation remains that biblical scholarship will be part of the group's study together. The expectation remains that each person's encounter with the Bible will call him or her to more faithful discipleship. In fact, it is our hope that this series of short-term DISCIPLE Bible studies will ultimately inspire participants to commit to a long-term DISCIPLE study in the future. For while these short studies of selected Scriptures can be both meaningful and convenient, the deeply transforming experience of reading and studying all the Scriptures—from Genesis to Revelation—continues to be the primary aim of DISCIPLE.

Leading This Study

For leaders of INVITATION TO ROMANS, it will be vital to keep in mind that to have as rich and meaningful an experience as possible with this type of short-term study, you will need to pay close attention to the timing of the suggested discussion activities and group dynamics. One of the challenges of any short-term, small-group study—especially one based on group discussion—is the time it takes for people in the study to become comfortable sharing with one another. If your group is made up of people who are already acquainted, the challenge may be minimal. However, be prepared to have a group of people who do not know each other well, perhaps some who have never done much substantive Bible study and others who are graduates of long-term DISCIPLE studies. Different challenges—and rewards—will come as a result of the mix of people who make up your group(s). Make use of the following information as you prepare to lead INVITATION TO ROMANS.

GROUP ORIENTATION

Plan to schedule an orientation meeting a week prior to the first weekly meeting. Take time then to make introductions, discuss the expectations of the study, distribute and review the materials, and preview the upcoming week's assignment. If necessary, consider discussing the kind of study Bible group members should use and taking time to make sure everyone is familiar with the aids in a study Bible. Have on hand several types of study Bibles for persons to look through.

WEEKLY SESSION

The times in parentheses beneath each section heading in the leader guide planning pages indicate the suggested number of minutes to allow for a particular activity. The first time is for use with a 60-minute meeting schedule, and the second time is for use with a 90-minute meeting schedule. Keep in mind that the discussion questions suggested for use in any one section may be more than enough to take up the allotted time. You will need to keep an eye on a clock and decide when and whether to move on. **The best way to gauge in advance how many questions to use and how long to allow discussion to last is to spend time answering the suggested questions yourself while preparing for the group session.** Be sure to do this, as well as preview the video—both Part 1 and 2—before the weekly session.

Gathering Around God's Word

(15–20 minutes)

Welcome

Begin on time by welcoming the group to the study. Ideally, this should be the *second* time the group has been together. During the orientation meeting the previous week, group participants met to preview the materials, discuss expectations of the study, and receive the assignment for the week. In case group participants arrive at this first session who were not present at the orientation meeting, be prepared to summarize as briefly as possible what they can expect from the study and what the study will expect from them.

Prayer

Establish a particular ritual of praying together at the start of the study. Keep in mind that the text of this study—the Bible—is a rich source of meaningful prayers. When appropriate, make use of other Bible translations when praying the Scriptures. Consider passages from the Book of Romans for use when praying together: for example, Romans 8:38-39; 11:33-36; 15:13; 16:25-27.

Hymn of Invitation (Optional)

Hymn writers throughout the ages have found in the Book of Romans inspiration for composing songs for the church to sing in worship. Consider singing or reading together the words of a hymn relating to the week's session. You may use the one suggested on the planning page, or you may choose another.

Viewing the Video: Session 1, Part 1

The video component in the series has two parts, and both are central to the group's study. Part 1 includes a narrative presentation of a key portion of the Scripture read in each lesson, followed by a brief conversation between two scholars. This video segment is designed to: (1) help the group experience how a gathering of early Christians might have heard Paul's letter and (2) invite reflection and discussion of the message of the text. Hearing Scripture spoken aloud will often highlight a word or phrase that generates fresh insight into a familiar text. Encourage your group to be alert to that possibility.

Encountering God's Word in the Text

(20–25 minutes)

In this section, group discussion centers on the assigned Scripture passages read and studied during the week.

Examining God's Word in Context

(15–20 minutes)

Viewing the Video: Session 1, Part 2

The focus in this section is on viewing Part 2 of the video, which highlights some of the impact Paul's Letter to the Romans has had over the centuries. Michael Williams presents historical snapshots of people's encounter with Romans as a starting point for the group to talk about the continuing legacy of Paul's letter.

Going Forth With God's Word: An Invitation to Discipleship

(10–15 minutes)

Consideration of the implications of the week's readings for Christian discipleship is the point of this section. The discussion questions in the leader guide for each session come from questions raised in the commentary and the "For Reflection" sections of the participant book. Be alert to additional questions that come to mind and might be useful at this time in the group meeting. As with any of these discussion questions, some will work better than others, and some will take more time to answer than others. Given the time frame for your weekly meeting, you may not have time to work through all the questions in the leader guide. Choose those you think will work best for your group, or make up your own.

Closing and Prayer

Turn to the next session and preview the lesson and assignments for the week ahead. Establish a pattern of inviting prayer concerns and praying together at this time.

GROUP DYNAMICS

The effectiveness of the group's study together depends heavily upon the way you as the leader manage individual participation. Plan for the majority of the weekly discussion to take place in smaller groups of two to four. Smaller groupings will give everyone more opportunity to talk and are the best way for people to get to know one another quickly. They also reduce the possibility that a couple of people will dominate the conversation or that some will not contribute at all. Smaller groupings communicate that preparation is expected and essential for fruitful discussion.

Also key to the effectiveness of the group's study together is how you manage your role as the leader. Remember that your primary role is to facilitate the process, not to provide the information. To that end, follow these basic guidelines as you lead the study:

- Prepare exactly as participants would prepare; see yourself as a learner among learners.

- Know where the discussion is heading from the outset; this will minimize the chances of getting sidetracked along the way.

- Set ground rules for group participation and maintenance early on; doing so will encourage the whole group to take responsibility for monitoring itself.

- Be a good listener; don't be afraid of silence. Allow time for people to think before responding.

Additional Resources

Your group will need only the Bible and the participant book to have a meaningful experience with this study. However, if your group should encounter unfamiliar terms and concepts or would like more information about some biblical text or topic, be prepared to suggest or to bring in additional reference materials for them to use. You may choose to include additional research or study activities in your plan for the weekly meeting, or you may assign group members to make use of these other reference materials outside of the meeting time and to report briefly to the group.

Several resources—including versions in print, CD-ROM, and video—are recommended as follows:

Bibles

One of the ways to enhance people's reading and understanding of the Bible is to have them read from more than one translation. Plan to have several study Bible versions available in the meeting room. In addition, encourage your group to read the Bible with curiosity, to ask *Who? What? Where? When? How?* and *Why?* as they read. Remind your group to let the Scripture speak for itself, even if the apparent meaning is troubling or unclear. Affirm both asking questions of Scripture as well as seeking answers to those questions in Scripture itself.

For this study of Romans in particular, a study Bible that includes the Apocrypha will be useful. The Apocrypha is a term used to describe the collection of Old Testament books considered canonical by Catholic and Orthodox churches but noncanonical by Protestants and Jews.

Bible Dictionaries
- *Eerdmans Dictionary of the Bible,* edited by David Noel Freedman (Wm. B. Eerdmans Publishing Company, 2000).

- *The HarperCollins Bible Dictionary,* edited by Paul J. Achtemeier (HarperSanFrancisco, 1996).

Introductory Resources
- *Introducing the New Testament: Its Literature and Theology,* by Paul J. Achtemeier, Joel B. Green, and Marianne Meye Thompson (Wm. B. Eerdmans Publishing Company, 2001).

- *Dictionary of Paul and His Letters*, edited by Gerald F. Hawthorne, Ralph P. Martin, and Daniel G. Reid (InterVarsity Press, 1993).

- *Final Account: Paul's Letter to the Romans*, by Krister Stendahl (Augsburg Fortress, 1995).

- *The Theology of Paul the Apostle*, by James D. G. Dunn (Wm. B. Eerdmans Publishing Co., 1998).

Biblical Commentaries

- *The New Interpreter's Bible: A Commentary in Twelve Volumes* (Abingdon Press, 1995–2002). Also available in a CD-ROM edition.

- *Eerdmans Commentary on the Bible*, edited by James D. G. Dunn and John W. Rogerson (William B. Eerdmans Publishing Company, 2003).

- *Ancient Christian Commentary on Scripture, New Testament VI: Romans*, edited by Gerald Bray (InterVarsity Press, 1998).

- *Romans*, in Interpretation: A Bible Commentary for Teaching and Preaching, by Paul J. Achtemeier (John Knox Press, 1985).

- *Romans in Full Circle: A History of Interpretation*, by Mark Reasoner (Westminster John Knox Press, 2005).

Art and Archaeology Related to the Bible

- *Archaeological Study Bible*, New International Version (The Zondervan Corporation, 2005).

- *The Biblical World in Pictures*, revised edition, CD-ROM (Biblical Archaeological Society).

- *The Bible and the Land: In Context*, DVD (Preserving Bible Times, Inc., 2003). For more information, go to http://www.preservingbible-times.org/content1.asp and click on "DVD Products."

An Orientation to Romans

Gathering Around God's Word

(15–20 minutes)

Welcome

Begin on time by welcoming the group to the study. Ideally this should be the second time the group has been together. During the orientation meeting the previous week, group participants met to preview the materials, discuss expectations of the study, and receive the assignment for the week. In case group participants who were not present at the orientation meeting arrive at the first session, be prepared to summarize as briefly as possible what they can expect from the study and what the study will expect from them.

Prayer

Establish a particular ritual of praying together at the start of the study. Keep in mind that the text of this study—the Bible—is a rich source of meaningful prayers. When appropriate, make use of other Bible translations when praying the Scriptures. Consider passages from the Book of Romans for use when praying together: for example, Romans 8:38-39; 11:33-36; 15:13; 16:25-27.

Hymn of Invitation (Optional)

Hymn writers throughout the ages have found in the Book of Romans inspiration for composing songs for the church to sing in worship. Consider singing or reading together the words of a hymn relating to the week's session. Suggestion: "How Firm a Foundation."

Viewing the Video: Session 1, Part 1

The video component in the series has two parts, and both are central to the group's study. Part 1 includes a narrative presentation of a key portion of the Scripture read in each lesson, followed by a brief conversation between two scholars. This video segment is designed to: (1) help the group experience how a gathering of early Christians might have heard Paul's letter and (2) invite reflection and discussion of the message of the text. Hearing Scripture spoken aloud will often highlight a word or phrase that generates fresh insight into a familiar text. Encourage your group to be alert to that possibility.

Prepare to View Video:
Listen carefully to portions of the opening and closing chapters of Romans. Note Paul's description of himself and his purpose for writing to those in Rome, as well as what he says about the character of God. The discussion between the two scholars centers on Romans as a source of tension for its many interpreters.

Discuss After Viewing Video:
• What new insights did you gain from hearing the passages from Romans spoken aloud?

• What main message do you think the community of believers in first-century Rome heard in these words of Paul?

• How have you known or experienced a passage in the Book of Romans to be a source of tension, conflict, or controversy, particularly with regard to the nature of God?

• Recall Mark Reasoner's comment that third-century theologian Origen thought Romans was about "how God's good news of Jesus goes for Jews and non-Jews; it goes for the world." What are the implications of that statement in terms of our twenty-first-century world?

Encountering God's Word in the Text

(20–25 minutes)

A primary emphasis in Romans is the character of God. Discuss the picture of God that comes from the assigned readings for Day 1 and Day 2 by forming three groups. Assign one group Deuteronomy 4:1-40, a second group Isaiah 40:1–41:10, and a third group Romans 1. Have each group scan and review notes made on the assigned passage, and then discuss together this question:

• According to this Scripture, who is God?

Another key emphasis in Romans is the contrast between the righteous character of God and the idolatrous nature of humankind. Have someone read aloud Wisdom of Solomon 14:8-11, 27-31, followed by Romans 1:18-25. Listen for what is said about idolatry. Then discuss these questions:

- What is idolatry? What makes idolatry such a defining characteristic of humankind, at least from the Bible's point of view?

- What does Paul accomplish by addressing the traditional biblical theme of idolatry at the start of his letter?

Recall what you learned about Paul himself from Romans 1 (Day 1) and Galatians 1 (Day 4). As a total group, share responses to the question under the Day 4 assignment: "In what ways does Paul's Damascus road experience resemble (or not) the call of Israel's most celebrated prophets?" Then consider these additional questions:

- How might seeing Paul's Damascus road experience more as a prophetic calling than as a conversion provide insight into his message in Romans?

- Would you describe the origins of your faith story as a sense of "calling," as an experience of "conversion," or as something else? Explain.

Examining God's Word in Context

(15–20 minutes)

Christians often come to Paul's Letter to the Romans with the expectation that it is as complete and unified an expression of the Christian faith as there is in the New Testament. In truth, Romans has proved to be one of the more challenging biblical texts for lay students and scholars to grasp fully. In fact, the history of the interpretation of Romans has only confirmed how often through the centuries Paul's message has been understood in various and sometimes contradictory ways. Like ten people viewing the same sunset but each coming away with a different take on it, so Romans has been a singular source of inspiration for Christians, yet prompting a wide array of perspectives.

Viewing the Video: Session 1, Part 2

The focus in this section is on viewing Part 2 of the video, which highlights some of the impact Paul's Letter to the Romans has had over the centuries. Michael Williams presents historical snapshots of people's encounter with Romans as a starting point for the group to talk about the continuing legacy of Paul's letter.

Prepare to View Video:
Listen for what is said about the broad and varied impact Romans has had on the church and some of its major figures, particularly Martin Luther and John Wesley.

Discuss After Viewing Video:
- What do you see when you come to the Book of Romans? What one word, phrase, or verse comes to mind?

- What is it in your reading of Romans that has caused your heart to be "strangely warmed"?

- What key teaching(s) of the church do you associate with or attribute to a passage in Romans? What key teaching(s) of the church do you not find in Romans?

Going Forth With God's Word: An Invitation to Discipleship

(10–15 minutes)

The two most important categories for understanding Paul's message in Romans are Jews and Gentiles. According to Paul, the main difference between Jews and Gentiles is that Gentiles do not know the one, true, living God, making them idolaters. So early on, Paul's message includes teaching Gentiles just who this one God of Israel is.

Talk together about why Paul considers it important to establish who God is before addressing who Jesus Christ is. Then recall the paragraphs under the "Invitation to Discipleship" section on page 24 of the participant book and consider the two invitations from Paul identified there: 1) to understand the profound chasm between human nature and God's nature and 2) to hear and believe the "gospel of God" and to take that gospel to the nations. In pairs, discuss how Christian believers today can (and do) respond to those two invitations.

Conclude the group's discussion by calling attention to the "For Reflection" section on page 25 in the participant book. Share responses to the question in the second bullet in that section.

Closing and Prayer

Turn to Session 2. Review the focus of the lesson and the assignments for the week ahead. Establish a pattern of inviting prayer concerns and praying together at this time. Also, consider singing the hymn of invitation mentioned earlier (page 13) as part of the closing along with or instead of using it as part of the opening.

The Righteousness of God and the Faith of Jesus

Gathering Around God's Word

(15–20 minutes)

Welcome
Begin on time by welcoming the group to the study.

Prayer
Pray together as you begin your study.

Hymn of Invitation (Optional)
Consider singing or reading together the words of a hymn relating to the week's session. Suggestion: "Immortal, Invisible, God Only Wise."

Viewing the Video: Session 2, Part 1

Prepare to View Video:
Listen to the reading from Romans 2 and 3. Pay attention especially to the phrases that include the words *law, faithfulness,* and *righteousness.* The discussion between the two scholars centers on how Origen and Luther defined *righteousness.*

Discuss After Viewing Video:
• What new insights did you gain from hearing the passages from Romans spoken aloud? To what extent did hearing the Scripture presented as a conversation between two speakers illuminate some aspect of the text?

• What main message do you think the community of believers in first-century Rome heard in these words of Paul?

• Which definition of *righteousness*—Origen's (a virtue) or Luther's (a label)—do you think comes closest to Paul's meaning? On which definition do you think Christians today base their faith?

- Where do you see the ripple effect of Paul's notion of righteousness in our world today? How is the church being (or not being) a vehicle of God's justice or righteousness beyond its own institutional boundaries?

Encountering God's Word in the Text

(20–25 minutes)

Whenever Paul specifies the direction toward which human faith should be focused, it is always toward God—a God who is righteous. Form groups of three or four to discuss the week's Scripture readings in Deuteronomy (Day 1) and in Psalms (Day 4). Have the groups summarize and talk about what these passages say about the righteousness of God and how humankind is to relate to a righteous God. Then focus on Romans 2–3 and discuss the following questions:

- Why do you think it is important for Paul to establish not only that God is righteous but also that God's judgment on human sin (Romans 2:2-5) is righteous?

- What do you make of what Paul says in Romans 2:9-10? How do you understand the relationship between our accountability before God and our faith in God?

- What does Paul mean by saying that "a person is a Jew who is one inwardly" (Romans 2:29)?

- In Romans 3:5, the Greek phrase translated in the NRSV as "justice of God" is the same Greek phrase translated as "righteousness of God" earlier in 1:17. How are God's "justice" and God's "righteousness" one and the same?

As noted on pages 34–35 in the commentary section of the participant book, the question of how to translate Romans 3:22 and 26 has been around for a long time and carries significant theological implications. Listen to Romans 3:21-31 read aloud from an NRSV Bible. Then, as a total group, discuss these questions:

- What do you think Paul was trying to say in this passage?

- How would you define *justification by faith*?

- What role do works play in faith?

- What is at stake in understanding God's righteousness disclosed through the faith *of* Jesus rather than through faith *in* Jesus Christ?

Examining God's Word in Context

(15–20 minutes)

We can participate in God's gift of righteousness as we respond in faith to the faithful obedience that Jesus Christ showed to God through his life, death, and resurrection.

Viewing the Video: Session 2, Part 2

Prepare to View Video:
Listen for what is said about Jonathan Edward's perspective on the righteousness of God.

Discuss After Viewing Video:
Michael Williams mentions the titles of three sermons or treatises by the Puritan Jonathan Edwards: "Sinners in the Hands of an Angry God," "The Justice of God in the Damnation of Sinners," and "A Faithful Narrative of the Surprising Work of God."

- When have you heard sermons with similar titles or similar themes? How did they affect you?

- What value do you see in acknowledging both the reality of human depravity and our utter and undeserving dependence upon God's mercy?

- What is it about God's righteousness that can point individuals to God's grace?

Going Forth With God's Word: An Invitation to Discipleship

(10–15 minutes)

We are all held accountable to the law of God but not made righteous by that law. It is only through God's intervention and grace that we can be justified and receive the righteousness of God. In pairs, discuss the following question:

- What does it mean to "live (as righteously as we can) by faith" (participant book, page 36)?

Conclude the group's discussion by calling attention to the "For Reflection" section on page 37 in the participant book. Ask the group to form pairs and share responses to the third bulleted set of questions in that section. Then continue the discussion using these questions:

- To what extent do we see salvation as dependent upon our own faithful obedience?

- To what extent do we see salvation as dependent upon Jesus' faithful obedience?

Closing and Prayer

Turn to Session 3. Review the focus of the lesson and the assignments for the week ahead. Consider singing the hymn of invitation mentioned earlier (page 18) as part of the closing along with or instead of using it as part of the opening. Close with prayer.

Abraham, Father of All

Gathering Around God's Word

(15–20 minutes)

Welcome
Begin on time by welcoming the group to the study.

Prayer
Pray together as you begin your study.

Hymn of Invitation (Optional)
Consider singing or reading together the words of a hymn relating to the week's session. Suggestion: "O God, Our Help in Ages Past."

Viewing the Video: Session 3, Part 1

Prepare to View Video:
Listen to the reading from Romans 4 and 5. Note what we as heirs of Abraham have received and will receive. The discussion between the two scholars centers on issues that arise from seeing the Abraham connection Paul emphasizes between Gentiles and Jews.

Discuss After Viewing Video:
- What new insights did you gain from hearing the passages from Romans spoken aloud? How do Paul's words strike you—as a challenge, as a comfort, or as something else?

- What main message do you think the community of believers in first-century Rome heard in these words of Paul?

- Why do you think the church, in spite of these passages in Romans, still has not come to terms with the Jewishness of Jesus?

Discuss some examples in our world today of how the common ancestry of Abraham among Judaism, Islam, and Christianity serves as a source both of unity and division.

Encountering God's Word in the Text

(20–25 minutes)

Central to understanding Paul's argument in this week's readings is understanding who Abraham is and what God's promise to Abraham entails. In the total group, take time to recall briefly the story of Abraham in Genesis 15:1–18:15; 21:1-21 in order to identify what characterizes Abraham and his relationship to God.

Then alert the group to page 44 in the participant book, where the writer of the commentary section translates the opening question in Romans 4:1 as "What then shall we say? Have we found Abraham to be our ancestor according to the flesh?" Then, on page 45, she declares, "Absolutely not! Abraham is the ancestor of God's people according to the promise." Just as Paul does in Galatians, here in Romans 4 he boldly claims that Abraham is the father of Jews and Gentiles alike, thanks to God's promise. Consider what it means for us to be present-day heirs to an ancient promise by first hearing these passages read aloud: Genesis 15:1-6; Galatians 3:6-9; and Romans 4:13-17. Then form groups of three or four to discuss these questions:

- As a Christian, what challenges do you confront in reading the story of Abraham as your story?

- What does Abraham and Sarah's participation in God's promise to Israel (through having Isaac) say about the nature of God's ultimate promise to all peoples and all of creation?

- What do you receive as an heir of Abraham? As an heir of Christ?

- What is your responsibility toward God as an heir?

Paul begins the opening paragraph of Romans 5:1-11 with a dramatic "therefore," signaling that what he has said thus far (about God's righteousness, human sinfulness, Abraham's faithfulness, and so on) supports what he is about to say.

- According to these eleven verses, what are the fruits of being justified by God?

- What exactly can we as Christians boast about in God (5:11)?

Finally, consider this question:

- If justification by faith is the answer, what is the question?

Examining God's Word in Context

(15–20 minutes)

Abraham is deemed righteous before he is circumcised. Abraham cannot have earned his righteousness; it is simply bestowed on him as a gift.

Viewing the Video: Session 3, Part 2

Prepare to View Video:
Listen for what is said about how John Calvin saw the relationship between the practices of circumcision and baptism.

Discuss after Viewing Video:
- How do you understand baptism as part of church practice? What does it symbolize for you and your congregation?

- How do you and your congregation work to break down the wall that separates Jew and Gentile (or Christian) today?

Going Forth With God's Word: An Invitation to Discipleship

(10–15 minutes)

Through the faithfulness of Abraham and the faithfulness of Jesus, all of creation is guided toward God's intended purpose. Likewise, our faith in God should guide us to carry out God's intended purpose not merely for ourselves but for all of creation.

In pairs, discuss the following questions:

- When have you responded to crisis or trial with the trust of Abraham?

- In what ways do you think your life of faith is helping carry out God's intended purposes in the world?

Conclude the group's discussion by calling attention to the "For Reflection" section on page 48 in the participant book. Still in pairs, share responses to the first two questions in that section.

Closing and Prayer

Turn to Session 4. Review the focus of the lesson and the assignments for the week ahead. Consider singing the hymn of invitation mentioned earlier (page 22) as part of the closing along with or instead of using it as part of the opening. Close with prayer.

Christ, the New Adam

Gathering Around God's Word

(15–20 minutes)

Welcome
Begin on time by welcoming the group to the study.

Prayer
Pray together as you begin your study.

Hymn of Invitation (Optional)
Consider singing or reading together the words of a hymn relating to the week's session. Suggestion: "Grace Greater Than Our Sin."

Viewing the Video: Session 4, Part 1
Adam is a type of human being who represents the entire race. Jesus is a new type of human being who "re-represents" the human race. What was lost in Adam is restored in Christ. So Christ is the new Adam.

Prepare to View Video:
Listen to the reading of portions of Romans 5 and 6 and pay attention to what Paul says about sin and grace. The discussion between the two scholars centers on the notion of original sin and the difference between the views of Augustine and Pelagius.

Discuss After Viewing Video:
- What new insights did you gain from hearing the passages from Romans spoken aloud? What contrasting words or phrases did you hear that stood out (for example, "death spread to all" and "grace abounded")?

- What main message do you think the community of believers in first-century Rome heard in these words of Paul?

- How have you experienced the sacraments of the church as a means of making you one with Christ, the new Adam?

- Would you say you lean toward Augustine (we are born sinful) or Pelagius (we choose to sin) in your understanding of original sin? Why? Where does your idea about original sin come from?

Encountering God's Word in the Text

(20–25 minutes)

The instructions in the daily reading assignments for Day 2 and Day 3 call attention to the analogy Paul draws between Adam and Christ, both in Romans and in 1 Corinthians 15. Invite persons to identify the similarities and differences in what Paul says about Adam and Christ in the two letters.

According to this week's readings, a key point Paul makes is to assert that being "in Adam" connects people to sin, while being "in Christ" connects people to justification. To address this line of Paul's argument, form two groups. Have one group focus on identifying the essential characteristics of Adam and the other group focus on identifying the essential characteristics of Christ. Once each group has completed its work, come together as a total group to discuss these questions:

- How does Paul see Adam's character shaping the world? How does Paul see Christ's character shaping the world?

- What are some of the consequences of our living essentially between two worlds: an Adam-shaped world and a Christ-shaped world?

Finally, listen to Philippians 2:1-18 read aloud. Discuss this question:

- If disobedience is a characteristic we share with Adam, what characteristic do we share with Christ?

Examining God's Word in Context

(15–20 minutes)

Viewing the Video: Session 4, Part 2

Prepare to View the Video:
Listen for what is said about Dietrich Bonhoeffer, his perspective on baptism, and his notion of costly grace.

Discuss After Viewing Video:
Read aloud Bonhoeffer's description of cheap grace from *The Cost of Discipleship*, cited in the video: "[It] is the preaching of forgiveness without

requiring repentance, baptism without church discipline, Communion without confession" (SCM Press Ltd, 1959; page 47). Then discuss these questions:

- To what extent has Bonhoeffer's notion of cheap grace ever been descriptive of your experience of congregational life?

- How have you found God's abounding grace also to be costly?

Going Forth With God's Word: An Invitation to Discipleship

(10–15 minutes)

Against a picture of Adam, Paul presents a picture of Christ. We see the paradox of two worlds: one that leads to sin and death, and one that leads to justification and life. In pairs, discuss the following question:

- What for you is the most pressing issue in trying to live with one foot in Adam's world and one foot in Christ's world?

Still in pairs, consider a statement in the final paragraph under the "Invitation to Discipleship" section on page 57 in the participant book: "Christ's one act has greater impact on us all than Adam's one act ever had." In terms of balance, God's gift of grace is tipped in our favor. With that in mind, discuss this question:

- Despite living as we do in a world that too often seems grim and without grace, how should receiving this overabundance of God's grace shape our discipleship?

Conclude the group's discussion by calling attention to the "For Reflection" section on page 58 in the participant book. In pairs, share responses to the questions in that section.

Closing and Prayer

Turn to Session 5. Review the focus of the lesson and the assignments for the week ahead. Consider singing the hymn of invitation mentioned earlier (page 25) as part of the closing along with or instead of using it as part of the opening. Close with prayer.

Sin, Law, and Grace

Gathering Around God's Word

(15–20 minutes)

Welcome
Begin on time by welcoming the group to the study.

Prayer
Pray together as you begin your study.

Hymn of Invitation (Optional)
Consider singing or reading together the words of a hymn relating to the week's session. Suggestion: "And Can It Be That I Should Gain" (stanza 5).

Viewing the Video: Session 5, Part 1

Prepare to View Video:
Listen to the reading from Romans 7 and 8. Pay attention to how the presentation of the Scripture as a dialogue between two speakers highlights aspects of the text. The discussion between the two scholars centers on what Paul means to say in Romans 7 about the Christian life and the nature of conversion.

Discuss After Viewing Video:
- What new insights did you gain from hearing the passages from Romans spoken aloud? At the close of the presentation, did you feel exhilarated or burdened? Why?

- What main message do you think the community of believers in first-century Rome heard in these words of Paul?

One of the questions raised in the scholars' conversation is "What is the nature of conversion?"

- How would you describe conversion? What do you think of Origen's belief that we are converted gradually? How does Luther's notion of being a sinner and justified at the same time fit into the idea of conversion?

- How would you describe the normal struggle of the Christian life?

Encountering God's Word in the Text

(20–25 minutes)

At issue in understanding this week's readings is addressing what the writer of the commentary calls the "default" reading of Romans 7—namely, the assumption that Paul is talking about himself and his own conversion. One way to approach this issue in the total group is to invite persons, one at a time, to summarize Paul's argument in Romans 7. Then listen to Romans 6:15-23 and 8:1-11 read aloud.

In light of hearing summaries of Romans 7 and the passages that come before and after that chapter, discuss these questions:

- What similarities are there between Romans 6:15-23 and Romans 1?

- How does Romans 6:15-23 set the stage for what Paul says in the following chapter?

- What is Paul saying in Romans 7 about the law? About sin? About the relationship between law and sin?

- If the problem for Paul is not the law, then what is the problem? Furthermore, how do we as Christians today experience that problem?

- How do we reconcile the freedom Paul celebrates in Romans 8:1-11 with the struggle he laments in Romans 7?

Examining God's Word in Context

(15–20 minutes)

Romans deals with the tension of law and grace and how one lives a Christian life in the midst of that tension.

Viewing the Video: Session 5, Part 2

Prepare to View Video:
Listen for what is said about the experiences of Augustine and missionary David Brainerd.

Discuss After Viewing Video:

- To what extent do you find it helpful to know that the saints of the church have agonized over their daily struggle in the flesh?

- In your own faith, when have you experienced the highs and lows of despairing in your own sinfulness and rejoicing in God's promises?

Both Augustine (*Confessions*) and David Brainerd (*Diary*) wrote about the highs and lows of their faith journeys. What value (for ourselves as well as for others) is there in keeping an ongoing record of our experience of Christian faith?

Going Forth With God's Word: An Invitation to Discipleship

(10–15 minutes)

Paul's charge to us is to live according to the Spirit and not gratify the desires of the flesh. The implied promise is that setting our minds on the things of the Spirit will lead to life and peace. The struggles of life and the problem of sin and death will not be over, but we will be facing in the right direction. In pairs, discuss the following questions:

- Looking back over your life, would you say you live more often by the law or by grace? Why?

- How would you describe your relationship to God, more as a sense of obligation or as an act of love? Why?

Conclude the group's discussion by calling attention to the "For Reflection" section on page 68 in the participant book. Still in pairs, read aloud Galatians 5:16-26 and share responses to the last question in that section.

Closing and Prayer

Turn to Session 6. Review the focus of the lesson and the assignments for the week ahead. Consider singing the hymn of invitation mentioned earlier (page 28) as part of the closing along with or instead of using it as part of the opening. Close with prayer.

Divine Purpose and Human Responsibility

Gathering Around God's Word

(15–20 minutes)

Welcome
Begin on time by welcoming the group to the study.

Prayer
Pray together as you begin your study.

Hymn of Invitation (Optional)
Consider singing or reading together the words of a hymn relating to the week's session. Suggestion: "O Love That Wilt Not Let Me Go."

Viewing the Video: Session 6, Part 1

Prepare to View Video:
Listen to the reading from Roman 9. Notice the emphasis on purpose and promise. The discussion between the two scholars centers on the idea of predestination in Romans.

Discuss After Viewing Video:
- What new insights did you gain from hearing the passages from Romans spoken aloud?

- What main message do you think the community of believers in first-century Rome heard in these words of Paul?

- What would you say to someone who came to you and questioned his or her salvation? How have you confronted the difficulty of making sense of the doctrine of predestination?

- What do you think of Mark Reasoner's suggestion to see predestination language as the "thankful language of someone looking back at all that happened"?

Encountering God's Word in the Text

(20–25 minutes)

Approach this week's readings in two ways. First, consider Paul's lyric celebration of Christian hope found in Romans 8. Form three groups and assign them these passages:

Group 1—Romans 8:18-27

Group 2—Romans 8:28-30

Group 3—Romans 8:31-39

Ask each group to read the assigned passage and compose a brief declaration of faith to complete this sentence: "We rejoice in hope because...." Once the groups complete the assignment, listen to the three declarations read aloud.

Then, as a total group, share responses to the question posed in the daily reading assignment section for Day 2 on page 70 in the participant book:

- How does Paul's emphasis on the unfailing love of God here relate to the wrath of God that he forecast in Romans 1?

Next, focus on the assigned reading from Romans 9, particularly the theme of "God's purpose of election" (9:11). To begin with, recall the readings from Genesis and Job and talk about how they support or provide insight into what Paul says about how and whom God chooses. Then discuss these questions around the idea of human free will and divine election:

- How does Paul depict God in Romans 9?

- Based on your reading of Romans thus far, how would you define *God's purpose of election*?

- What does Paul mean to say in Romans 9:22-24?

The Roman coin graphic in the margin of page 76 in the participant book contains a statement about Origen's position regarding free will. Go around the group and hear how persons respond to it.

Examining God's Word in Context

(15–20 minutes)

God takes the initiative in calling people, but people have a part to play in working toward salvation. Those who are called choose either to respond in faithful obedience or to resist; but the choice is theirs to make.

Viewing the Video, Session 6, Part 2

Prepare to View Video:
Listen for what is said about Luther and Erasmus and their conflicting views regarding the nature of God and human free will.

Discuss After Viewing Video:
- How does your image of God inform or shape your thoughts about salvation?

- How does your image of God inform or shape your thoughts about divine purpose and human responsibility?

- If you had to choose between the view of human will championed by Luther or by Erasmus, which would you choose and why?

Going Forth With God's Word: An Invitation to Discipleship

(10–15 minutes)

God is still active in the world today and desires to be in relationship with God's creation. Conversely, we seek out God's presence and activity in the events of our lives and desire to be in relationship with God.

Call attention to the "For Reflection" section on page 78 in the participant book. Invite pairs to share responses to the questions in that section.

Closing and Prayer

Turn to Session 7. Review the focus of the lesson and the assignments for the week ahead. Consider singing the hymn of invitation mentioned earlier (page 31) as part of the closing along with or instead of using it as part of the opening. Close with prayer.

The Salvation of Israel and the Nations

(15–20 minutes)

Welcome
Begin on time by welcoming the group to the study.

Prayer
Pray together as you begin your study.

Hymn of Invitation (Optional)
Consider singing or reading together the words of a hymn relating to the week's session. Suggestion: "How Shall They Hear the Word of God."

Viewing the Video: Session 7, Part 1

Prepare to View Video:
Listen to the reading of part of Romans 11. Note how the image of two olive trees is used to portray the salvation of Israel and the nations. The discussion between the two scholars centers on what Paul says about the Jews in Romans 9–11.

Discuss After Viewing Video:
- What new insights did you gain from hearing the passages from Romans spoken aloud?

- What main message do you think the community of believers in first-century Rome heard in these words of Paul?

- Mark Reasoner says that how the church reads this section of Romans affects how the church treats Israel. How is that true today?

- Bill Leonard observes that the church's discussion of Israel is shaped by theories of Christ's return. How is that true today?

Encountering God's Word in the Text

(20–25 minutes)

Work through the assigned readings in Romans by exploring the question posed in the commentary introduction on page 80 of the participant book:

- What is Israel's role now that Christ has come, now that a new age is dawning, an age in which Gentiles will also become part of God's family?

To do this, first get a sense of how the Old Testament defines Israel's role in God's purposes. Recall the assigned readings from the prophets for Day 1 and Day 4, and use these questions to guide discussion:

- What is the purpose of God having a specially chosen people?

- If God is God of the whole world, why would God distinguish Israel from other nations?

Then examine how Paul defines Israel's role in God's purpose. Form groups of three or four. Ask them to recall the week's readings from Romans and discuss these questions:

- What does Paul think is Israel's purpose as God's chosen people? What does Paul think is Israel's failure as God's chosen people?

- What does Paul think is God's response to Israel's failure? What does Paul think God accomplishes through Christ?

According to the commentary writer, "the scenario Paul describes in Romans 11 views Israel and the Gentile nations as mutually interdependent. Each needs the other in order for the world to be reconciled to God" (participant book, page 85).

- What are the implications of that statement for understanding the church's purpose today?

Finally, if time allows, listen to Romans 11:11-24 read aloud. Talk about the message conveyed by Paul's image of the wild and cultivated olive trees.

Examining God's Word in Context

(15–20 minutes)

Viewing the Video: Session 7, Part 2

Prepare to View Video:
Listen for what is said about William Carey and the rise of the modern missionary movement.

Discuss After Viewing Video:

• How do you think the church in this age reads and appropriates Romans 10:14-17?

• What does it mean for the church to be "duty-bound" to carry the gospel to all the world in the twenty-first century?

• What theological barriers, like the ones encountered by Carey, do missionaries face today?

Going Forth With God's Word: An Invitation to Discipleship

(10–15 minutes)

As agents of God's redemption, we are called to think not only of our own salvation but also the salvation and redemption of others. As a total group, discuss the following question:

• What response does Paul's broad vision of redemption call for from Christians today?

Turn to page 87 in the participant book and have someone read the statement in the Roman coin graphic in the right margin: "Paul sees salvation not as a matter to be worked out between each individual and God; he sees it as communal and cosmic. Salvation is a synonym for the redemption of the world." Discuss the group's responses to that idea.

Conclude the group's discussion by calling attention to the "For Reflection" section on page 89 in the participant book. Form pairs and share responses to the last two bulleted sets of questions in that section.

Closing and Prayer

Turn to Session 8. Review the focus of the lesson and the assignments for the week ahead. Consider singing the hymn of invitation mentioned earlier (page 34) as part of the closing along with or instead of using it as part of the opening. Close with prayer.

Love and Humility Are the Making of God's Kingdom

Gathering Around God's Word

(15–20 minutes)

Welcome
Begin on time by welcoming the group to the study.

Prayer
Pray together as you begin your study.

Hymn of Invitation (Optional)
Consider singing or reading together the words of a hymn relating to the week's session. Suggestion: "The Gift of Love."

Viewing the Video, Session 8, Part 1

Prepare to View Video:
Listen to the reading from Romans 12, 13, and 15. Pay attention to Paul's tone throughout, especially when he advocates a particular stance toward the governing authorities. The discussion between the two scholars centers on ways to interpret Romans 13:1-7.

Discuss After Viewing Video:
• What new insights did you gain from hearing the passages from Romans spoken aloud?

• What main message do you think the community of believers in first-century Rome heard in these words of Paul?

Apparently Origen's and Luther's interpretations of Romans 13:1-7 were shaped to some extent by their respective life situations relative to "governing authorities."

• To what extent do we view a text like this as a kind of "fair-weather" passage?

• When does the issue of religious liberty come up against the power of the state in our day? What is the church's response? To what Scriptures (besides Romans 13:1-7) does the church appeal when deciding how to relate to the state?

Encountering God's Word in the Text

(20–25 minutes)

The goal of love is to treat others so as always to build them up, even if those same people have acted in such a way as to tear us down. In groups of three or four, scan through the readings for Day 1 and Day 2. Using notes from personal study, compare the teachings of the law with the teachings of Paul. Discuss the following questions:

- What actions and attitudes does the law call for among the people of Israel?
- What actions and attitudes does Paul call for among the Christian community in Rome?
- In what ways is love the fulfilling of the law?

Read aloud Isaiah 55:1–56:8. In the total group, discuss the prophet's invitation to abundant life.

- Who is invited? To what are they invited?
- How does Paul's vision of salvation relate to Isaiah's vision of salvation?
- How can Paul's teachings in Romans 12–15 lead to the abundant life imagined by Isaiah?

If time allows, take up the issue of the "weak" and the "strong" in Romans 14:1–15:13. While it may be helpful to spend some time discussing who the weak and the strong might be, a more fruitful line of inquiry might result from addressing these questions:

- When have you been one of the strong in faith and practice and acted judgmentally toward one of the weak?
- When have you experienced the church (perhaps even your particular congregation) acting as the strong in judgment of the weak?

Examining God's Word in Context

(15–20 minutes)

Certainly Paul had his share of confrontations with the governing authorities. However, it is highly unlikely that Paul would have condoned submission to political officials if it meant committing idolatry.

Viewing the Video, Session 8, Part 2

Prepare to View Video:
Listen to what is said about Origen, Zwingli, and the Anabaptists and their responses to governing authorities.

Discuss After Viewing Video:
Name some other heroes of the faith known for their dissenting stance before governing authorities.

- What Scriptures informed their perspectives and actions?

- What guidelines do we use to hold ourselves accountable both to God and to our government?

- How far should we go in our allegiance to our country? When might we go too far and be guilty of idolatry?

Going Forth With God's Word: An Invitation to Discipleship

(10–15 minutes)

Paul's concluding words ring with urgency. He clearly expects the age of Christ to be coming soon. So he expects the Christians in Rome—and Christians today—to live toward the coming kingdom of God. Moreover, Paul's ethical teachings in these last chapters of Romans seem aimed to communicate at least one key idea: *Right actions matter more than right beliefs*. In pairs, discuss responses to that statement.

Conclude the group's discussion by calling attention to the "For Reflection" section on page 100 in the participant book. Still in pairs, share responses to the questions in that section.

Closing and Prayer

Thank the participants for their participation. Make any announcements that are needed. Consider singing the hymn of invitation mentioned earlier (page 37) as part of the closing along with or instead of using it as part of the opening. Close with prayer.

Video Art Credits

Portrait of St. Paul, by Pompeo Batoni. Basildon Park, Berkshire, Great Britain. National Trust / Art Resource, NY.

Martin Luther, by Lucas Cranach, the Elder (1472–1553 / German). Oil on Canvas. SuperStock, Inc.

John Wesley, by Nathaniel Hone I (1718–1784 / British). National Portrait Gallery, London. SuperStock, Inc.

Jonathan Edwards. Stock Montage, Inc. / SuperStock, Inc.

John Calvin. Stock Montage, Inc. / SuperStock, Inc.

Saint Augustine in His Study, by Sandro Botticelli (1444–1510 / Italian). Ognissanti Church, Florence, Italy. Bridgeman Art Library, London / SuperStock, Inc.

Dietrich Bonhoeffer Portrait. Hulton Archive / Getty Images.

CPSIA information can be obtained
at www.ICGtesting.com
Printed in the USA
LVOW10s2119100217

523924LV00008B/38/P